JAMAICA GALLERY

THE ARTIST–AUTHOR

Jamaica Gallery

Philip Kappel

INTRODUCTION BY JOHN P. MARQUAND

A DOCUMENTARY *of* THE ISLAND *of* JAMAICA, WEST INDIES

THE TEXT, DRAWINGS & DESIGNS *by* PHILIP KAPPEL

LITTLE, BROWN AND COMPANY · BOSTON · TORONTO

Address: The Caribbean

N

W cuba

Jamaica

E

S

Guadeloupe

Barbados

cartagena

South America

Trinidad

Colombia

INTRODUCTION

I HAVE known Philip Kappel since 1925, when, as a very young artist, he had a studio near the old Derby Wharf in Salem, Massachusetts. When he showed me some of his work in those early days, he demonstrated and explained to me the abstruse and difficult skills that go with the art of etching. In the course of his explanation, I remember that he showed me how nearly impossible it is in this medium to conceal or rectify an error. Thus one careless or misplaced line will always stand out to mar or obscure the ultimate result, no matter how excellent it may be.

Philip Kappel has made few or none of such mistakes, from that day to the present. Indeed, if he has made any error in technique, I am sure he has not been aware of it. If he had been, I have no doubt he would have destroyed his work, because there was never a more meticulous or painstaking craftsman in the difficult regions of etching, and the same may be said of his work in pen and ink, and pencil. Yet this determined desire for a technical perfection has never limited him as an artist. His adroitness with his media has, from almost the start of his distinguished career, been a matter of second nature. It has enhanced, instead of inhibited, his imagination. Actually his work is so seemingly free and effortless that its enormous skill is seldom immediately apparent to a casual observer. Instead, one is impressed by the depth and brilliance of his atmosphere. There is an illusion of sound and motion, of the heat of sun, of the welcome cool of shadow, and always contrast in all of the Kappel work.

Fortunately for his many admirers, Philip Kappel has always possessed the instincts of an inveterate traveler. Although he has a deep love and understanding of the sea, he was not content with the wharves and sailing vessels of New England. Anyone who has attended one of his exhibitions can see that his intuitive understanding of life and people has taken him to many strange and distant places. And no matter in what odd part of the world he may have paused, he has been artistically at home in it and in complete sympathy with its atmosphere and mood. To my way of thinking, the black-and-whites that he has collected in a volume entitled *Louisiana Gallery* give as graphically fine an impression of the deep South as *Huckleberry Finn* or the spirituals of its people. This collection of his Jamaica drawings will do the same for this romantically beautiful Caribbean island. Few people know Jamaica, particularly its unexploited areas, as well as Philip Kappel, and fewer still have been privileged to see it with his artistic sympathy. His Caribbean drawings have always given me great delight, not only because of their composition but because of their selectivity of detail. When you view these pictures of Jamaica, you are seeing this varied and still not overexploited island through the eyes of an outstanding artist. Somehow, whether you are an expert in the graphic arts or not, you know that you are in good hands and that Philip Kappel will communicate to you, through his medium, the spirit of Jamaica and its people.

JOHN P. MARQUAND
Kent's Island
Newburyport, Massachusetts

SINCE I am addicted to the charms of Jamaica, it is not surprising that for the ninth time in as many years, I was aboard one of those sleek aluminum-shod airliners going southward towards the Caribbean. A plane is no place for idle chatting with passengers; seldom does anyone nod and open a conversation, so the next best thing is to take all the free drinks and fall asleep.

When the plane approached Jamaica the loss in altitude became perceptible as the pilot probed a "hole" in the clouds in preparation for a landing on a mere geographical dot in the Caribbean. I was relieved and ebullient! The entire trip was uneventful and seemed slightly longer in flying time than a "cat nap," which I understand a "jet" could shorten considerably; dreamers lost in a "magic carpet" world will henceforth get less sleep.

Far below the plane the landing strip looked like a streak of white pigment on a verdant tapestry, beside a ruffled blue sea seared by the shadows of the clouds from which we planned to descend. The pilot quickly appraised the ceiling, banked the plane, and glided downward for a perfect landing. The landing gear struck the concrete with a slight thump and speedily rolled us towards the low airport buildings, where we smartly came to a halt.

With the motors dead, the silence inside the cabin was so pronounced that the trade winds began to sing in our ears. The passengers flew into action. The safety belts were thrown to one side, and the aisle became crowded with milling people adjusting wrinkled clothes and removing parcels from the racks. The inrushing tropical air rapidly filled the cabin and indoctrinated

Children on "Lalandia Beach" at Salem.

everyone into the delightful climate of Jamaica. Baggage inspection was brief. The official landing card was our carte blanche invitation to a carefree holiday. Passengers with prior hotel arrangements drove off in cars sent for them by multi-storied luxury hostelries with private beaches along the North Coast. Others went to simple hotels of their choice facing the sea, offering every potential for an easement into a world of relaxation and pleasure.

The minstrels at the airport stroll away into the cool shade when the tourists disappear, but the next arrival of a plane is greeted with vigor and enthusiasm. If it's atmosphere that the minstrels desire to inflict for coins, it goes without further emphasis that the confusion at an airport makes it the least desirable place for minstrels to strum calypsos. There it is for what it is worth. Every inch of spare room seems to be requisitioned by good and bad tempered people, friends of friends going places, and shoppers clustered around Free Port counters. Were it not for the restrictions placed on baggage, each departing plane for the states and elsewhere would have to be followed by a second plane carrying RUM. A good thing is seldom neglected for long and with centuries of Jamaican "know-how" behind sugar by-products, trial and error in quality is discounted. It's up to the purchaser to vindicate his investment, and in more ways than one, each sampling is worthy of its pleasant and consistent quality. If in doubt, leave Bay Rum alone. Keep it on the head—not in it. Rum and Bay Rum frequently sold from adjoining shelves happen to be conflicting do-gooders and must remain on opposite sides of the fence. Bay leaves and sugar cane have no "blood" ties.

Fishermen beaching their cotton tree canoe, and taking fish-pot to safety before the gathering storm.

PHILIP KAPPEL

Since I gave the taxi men no reason to look for me as a passenger, I had ample time to engage in a few idle moments of random thinking such as I have doted on, and like the errant child whisked off by an embarrassed parent for having said all the wrong things, I discovered that my charming friend with smiles of welcome was at the exit gate trying to catch my attention. The car was poised for the eighty-mile trip to the mountains and in short order I was perspiring among a motley assortment of baggage, wearing winter clothing that felt like medieval armor plate.

Leaving Montego Bay by the coastal road towards Ocho Rios kept the cooling breezes with us. Now and then we lost sight of the Caribbean when the luxuriant tropical growth obliterated it from view. Along the coast, mangroves and sea grape united in a common effort to hold the gnawing water in check. Wherever there is soil, however scanty, there are tall palms and squat banana trees or casuarinas bowing with the whims of the thrashing trades against a lapis lazuli sky. The mountains are in the background, and the plain through which we passed was so rich that numerous rotations of sugar cane ripened to extravagant heights. As we sped along, harvesters were slashing the cane with their machetes, and oxen or tractors were hauling away groaning loads to the mills. It was nip and tuck between the desire to linger for pictures or pressing on towards the next town. The longer we continued on our trip the more fascinating and varied the countryside became; it seemed like a land in constant motion—people everywhere were engaged in some occupation. If they were on foot they carried huge bundles on their heads with such grace they warranted a

Market day at Claremont. Buyers and sellers collect from far and wide by truck, mule-cart, and donkey.

Philip Kappel

second look. If on swaggering mules, much dignity prevailed in spite of sagging backs trying to sustain riders and baskets of produce for market. All of the passers-by were noncommunicative.

The entry into Ocho Rios was our first encounter with traffic problems. Our left lane was bogged down with pedestrians, carts drawn by donkeys, cars, frightened chickens, dogs, and children. The opposite lane was just as snarled.

With patience we were able, with some delay, to proceed into the road that turned away from the sea and towards fabulous Fern Gully. In retrospect, I am most appreciative of the picturesqueness of a coastal town in the tropics, but it is with misgivings that I am unable to shake from memory the boy on a bicycle beside the open window of our car, locked in traffic with us. He had on his head, exposed to the broiling sun, a load of fish going from somewhere to someplace! It isn't necessary to emphasize how long and unapplauded such uninvited titillation of the senses remained in deadlock and competition with a land so overwhelmingly steeped in jasmine and spices.

The drive through Fern Gully is an experience that remains sharp and piercing—a paragon of mystery and hypnosis. Twisting and turning like a serpent between lateral abutments of protruding rock, the road ascends the steep grade of the mountain with huge ferns alongside upon which the filtered sunshine falls as shafts of strangled light. The flora and the precipitous towering walls with their outcroppings of lichen and strange festoons of vines, dripping from recent showers, make the gully an awesome fantasy. The penetrating coolness of this eerie phenomenon is re-

Moneague Market. Confusion and bargaining at its height on a Saturday morning.

PHILIP KAPPEL

freshing—when we emerge into the brilliant sunshine again it seems uncommonly warm. We had come a long way from Montego Bay and time had evaporated significantly, so the next place should be Moneague.

Familiar landmarks appeared in rapid succession. The mountains looked tremendous and beautiful with quotas of cottonwood giants, cocoanut palms, and banana trees, and the sky a flurry of clouds racing towards the penetralia of dreams! Along the roadside, fences of blooming "quick-stick" defined the boundaries of the pens, and the scent of citrus and clean earth made the entry into Moneague unlike anything encountered so far. Catchments and thatch-roofed houses nestled in the hills made as beautiful and inviting a picture as any artist could hope to encounter—this was my kind of countryside; anyone could cut out a place for himself in it.

As soon as we turned away from the highway and into the dirt road that was to terminate our long drive, we heard the jubilant barking of the dogs as they gave delirious chase to the chickens to clear the yard for our "royal" entry. By the time the car reached the top of the conical hillock after a short corkscrew climb in low gear, the yard had been properly cleared; both dogs came bouncing forward to vigorously implant the seal of Moneague in mud on my clean city clothes.

In some magical manner my bags appeared in my sunny room; shortly thereafter an array of smiling faces came forward in the yard. It was henceforth my solemn duty to submit to their care. For someone who has had to make many of his own meals and

Roadside romance at Camperdown, St. Catherine; stone cutter astride her pile of stones coyly glances at her admirer.

keep his studio clean in the north, this was heaven; after pinching myself blue, I was indeed alive, so I jumped into a hot bath and took a shower with a calabash dipper. Refreshed and in comfortable clothes the preliminaries of the evening were concluded. A hasty examination of the "House on the Hill" impressed me. The off-white buildings, flooded by the light of the failing sun, gave the deep red poinsettia and bougainvillea unforgettable significance, and winter was by now too far away for comment.

The tinkle of ice in thin glasses aroused a responsive interest. It assured me that Jamaican hospitality had begun in earnest. The mesmerism of the present constricted a whole world of cares into a precious nugget of contentment.

The following day I had breakfast on the veranda facing the Diablo mountain range dramatically floating in mist; the morning began with pleasant anticipation. It was too early for the sun to drench the island with its warmth, but the withdrawing mist gradually gave the sun the chance to flood the land with shafts of sunshine that eventually expanded into a blanket across the island. Moneague began to stir into gradual crescendo.

The clarions of the dawn were village radios, dogs, and the musical horns on public conveyances announcing their approach into the village before continuing on towards Kingston. The chickens in the yard, too close to the forbidden veranda, were repeatedly chased from it by both dogs, but the young puppy who learned his manners from the older dog left behind a trail of feathers. His knowledge of watchdoggery was too slovenly administered to please anyone in the yard.

Helen Flynn with her peel at the oven in her yard at **Alderton.**

The kitchen performed its miracles with quiet demeanor—the tantalizing aroma of coffee and baking biscuits betrayed any false inactivity.

At the foot of the hill, the algae-covered pond is abandoned by the heron before the cows arrive for their morning drink, after their long descent from the mountain pasture. Before the sun has had a chance to climb appreciably over Mount Diablo, the nightingales had gone through their repertoire; the darting quits have had their temporary fill of careless bugs while the long-tailed humming birds made hasty visitations to the orange blossoms in the citrus tree by the veranda.

John Crow the scavenger, graceful in flight, suddenly glides down to reconnoitre near the veranda. I thought I noticed his shifty eyes fixed on me with moribund interest. Of course my composure was ruffled! How could he have known I was around, unless ——, and both dogs gave chase to the edge of the hilltop after him. I made a hasty mental inventory of my potentials for longevity. Notwithstanding the odds for or against me, and with the initiative still in my hands, I accepted Mr. John Crow's challenge. I threw out my chest and deeply inhaled the sweet-scented mountain air and stepped into the sunshine for a few rounds of vitamins. Breakfast by this time had appeared and it was eaten with defiant and retaliatory gusto!

The yard boy arrived from the village post office with the mail —it was approaching noon. He had stopped along the way to gossip but the delay did not warrant my impatience. There were many letters of welcome for me and my holiday was gaining momentum.

At "Montjoy" this ancient cedar tree covered with verdant parasites, wild pine, and orchids overlooks Scott Hill and the village of Moneague.

PHILIP KAPPEL

The early American ship owners cemented a bond of trade with friendship that endured.

PHILIP KAPPEL.

*T*HE itinerant tourist who expects to find the prototype of a small slumbrous place of isolation confutes his error before leaving the island of Jamaica. It is the largest island in the West Indies flying the Union Jack and is 144 miles long from east to west. Its greatest width is 49 miles from St. Ann's Bay on the north coast to Portland Point in the south.

Within this concentration of scenic pageantry there is a potpourri of dramatic and subtle charms amid severe territorial contrasts and social anachronisms! Superimposed upon all that is the expanding and encroaching prosperity that brought to Jamaica some unexpected changes, as well as many blessings. The mining of bauxite implanted a new look on the face of the island where nature left her deposits of valuable red clay. The tourist trade increased beyond any dream of the optimist, and the accelerated plane services made it easy to get away from winter in the north to bask in delightful sunshine on sandy beaches, unexcelled for their beauty. Hotels soon found their accommodations so shrunken to meet the demands for reservations that luxury hotels along the North Coast seemed to spring up between seasons. If one counts all the changes by old standards and comparisons, former impressions are outmoded by vast margins, and with all that concentrated activity it is surprising how untouched the rest of the island has resolved to remain. The grace of sugar cane in the fields, the lovely cocoanut trees, and the broad leaf banana contribute to the economic picture without altering the shape of the landscape; instead they beautify the zones wherever men have cast their lot in with nature's to bring something along to maturity.

Children at Barrett Hall; like most Jamaican children they win your affection with their searching curiosity.

PHILIP KAPPEL

From end to end the island is diversified; nothing the artist could do would be sustained as sufficient evidence of the breadth and magnanimity of the composition that stretches before his eyes. He plots and plans to bring the island into proper relationship with his medium, and piecemeal the island emerges, as if from a cocoon, to delight the eye or impart a singular message of enchantment that detained the artist long enough to record. It is the responsibility of the historian to give a good account of Jamaica's background—her conquerors and the conquered, plus the indelible scoring of their accomplishments—their impact and their furies, but try as we may to bypass them, the influence of the past upon the present often appears as the metamorphosis of their ambitions, and too often they are impossible to ignore.

The chief concern of the artist is with the romance of people and not with their bitterness.

As severe as the mountains of Jamaica are, their presence is felt with warm companionship. From every point of vantage distant peaks retain the setting sun long after the lowlands are wrapped in damp mists, and the incertitudes of the prowling nightfall are rent by the calls of tropical birds. In the eastern part of Jamaica the Blue Mountain Peak pierces the clouds at an altitude of 7,358 feet, and throughout the island the distribution of high places is something you are conscious of so long as you remain. Altitudes of 5,000 feet or slightly less are credible but commonplace, and the networks of roads—many began decades ago as footpaths—cut out of the solid rock are commendable for their brazen engineering skill. From the valleys the roads in many places look like rib-

The barbecue at Lucky Hill co-operative farm where dry chicken corn is measured and delivered to the car from "Montjoy."

PHILIP KAPPEL

bons on a Maypole clinging to the mountains in spirals of contorted consanguinity with the rising terrain. From east to west the ranges form a ridge across the island; down their slopes the rains sweep through rough ravines or cascade down steep rock formations until, as rivers, they emerge upon the open plains or lowlands flanked by thirsty tropical flora before entering the palm-fringed sea.

Kingston in the south and Montego Bay and Port Antonio on the other side of the mountains have much in common as ports of entry by boat or plane. The extremities of the island are connected by roads and telegraph. Modern traffic imposes many problems, and mountains are the least willing to co-operate with oversized trucks and public conveyances, donkeys, and pedestrians—all using the same narrow roads with twisting sharp curves. When the roads are wet, the hazards increase tenfold; a positive way to lose weight is to encounter a barrage of tourists in hired cars, squealing around the U turns high in the mountains.

On the less-travelled roads, hazards are at a minimum, but the surfaces are rough and of sharp stones. When pulverized, the wind blows them away and the rains wash whatever remains down the slopes. This necessitates constant attention and repairs. Dedicated to that service, whenever and wherever the need arises, large stockpiles of small stones are heaped along the sides of the secondary or Parochial roads. Women under shelters of banana or palm leaves are a common sight as they sit astride their piles of stone, making small stones from large chunks. They have a flair for the task but their hammers are handled with lethargic enthusiasm. In-

ROSEHALL

The tragedienne of St. James parish. Once the finest 18th century great house in the West Indies, now a gutted ruin brooding over the misdeeds of its former mistress, Rosa Palmer, a depraved specialist in lust, murder and indignities. Her badly treated slaves seized her one dark night and repaid her with torture and death.

PHILIP KAPPEL

variably, you can count on the tourist who happens to come upon such a serene composition of highway maintenance to erupt into phraseology that falls short of properly appreciating so delightful a picture. He's apt to make some reference to the efficiency of a stone crusher or some other kind of modern equipment that would ultimately rust away in disuse. Notwithstanding the array of suggestions from many quarters, just keeping people employed is a major victory on the island.

Not to be outdone by the mountains, the Caribbean, with its measurements in fathoms instead of feet, reverses the course of distances from height to depth. Outside the ring of reefs offshore in the north, the sea floor drops away to a low of 3,956 fathoms before rising to meet the beaches of Oriente Province in Cuba 90 miles away. It was across this barrier that the last of the Spaniards fled in small boats to Cuba from Jamaica. The victorious English inherited the task of revaluation, colonization, and consolidation. It was a herculean job—the marks were scored deep into the life stream of the island and the hands of many races shaped and moulded the image of their own destiny that succumbed to the will of English rule. And nature too adopted the soil of Jamaica—imported trees and seeds from faraway places grew with zealous determination to stay alive; those who would cultivate and care for the struggling seedlings discovered how profitable their ventures were. Today the fruits of the past continue to thrive and claim a stake in the prosperity of Jamaica.

Otherwise, few relics remain in Jamaica to testify for or against the kind of homes the early inhabitants had. As for their occupa-

Bankra basket maker transporting his wares on the road through Lydford, St. Ann.

tions and domestic habits, obscurity prevails. We have come to know something about the small copper-colored Indians—the Arawaks—who were the first to occupy the island; their stone artifacts left us a stinted story. Since they had no written language they left nothing but a legacy of mystery to provoke us; however, it is generously conceded by the experts that the Arawaks were a peace-loving people engaged in agricultural skills and it was their will to call the island they loved XAYMACA, "The Island of Springs." It was their misfortune to have their peace disturbed by the warlike invaders from the southern continent—the Caribs— against whom the Arawaks were no match. By the end of the sixteenth century, through abuse and slavery when the Spaniards held Jamaica, the Arawaks faded into legend. Christopher Columbus sailing south from Cuba in 1494 was well aware of Xaymaca and the possibility of finding gold on the island. Absurd as his assumption was, he returned the latter part of the year hoping to find it in abundance. His hopes and ambitions ended in disappointment and vexation. It is claimed that Columbus first called at St. Ann's Bay, which he called Santa Gloria, and the following day anchored at Rio Bueno, where he proclaimed the island Spanish in the name of the King and Queen of Spain. With or without gold, Spain thought well enough about Jamaica to send out its first governor in 1510; the honor fell upon Juan de Esquivel, the son of Columbus, who arrived with an accompaniment of troops and made a settlement at Seville, on the north coast. So many of them died from disease it became mandatory to transfer their headquarters from the north to the south, and establish them-

"Sea lace" drying on bamboo poles.
Salem fisherman mending his nets.

selves in 1534 where Spanish Town is located, 13 miles west of Kingston. The Spaniards called their capital St. Jago de La Vega.

Time ticked away and the years slipped into a buxom accumulation of monumental events. Ascending the Spanish throne in 1555, Philip II became the head of the most formidable nation in the entire world. Her possessions were far-flung and extensive; Spain represented might. She controlled islands in the Caribbean and the lands that ringed most of it, bearing the sobriquet "The Spanish Main." It was destined to come to the attention of nefarious bounders, pirates, and troublemakers by any other name. It was also going to get into the hair of ambitious rulers who controlled many nations, and directly or indirectly Jamaica was going to feel the "squeeze."

Proud sailing ships headed for Spain from Cartagena, Colombia, which was considered well fortified and impregnable. Her ships carried in their holds fabulous riches extorted from suppressed people; Spain was well aware of the risks involved when her shipping entered the open sea, and the buccaneers lost little time mulling over the moral aspects of relieving Spain of some of the chattels that might endanger her overloaded ships in storms. Such facetiousness met with little appreciation from Spanish captains who had sworn to make a safe landfall in Spain. Extra crews gave the swaggering bloodthirsty vermin of the high seas a hard time whenever they boarded Spanish vessels, but the dexterity of the buccaneers was no small ballroom maneuver—a cutlass in the hands of determined highjackers made the distance outside of a slashing blade an orbit of commendable latitude. The unfortunates

Mail being distributed at the old Claremont post office, recently replaced by a more imposing building nearby.

who fared poorly on their way to Spain had little to recommend their swordsmanship as they sank to "Davy Jones' locker."

Yes! Piracy had reasonable dangers, but the brilliant picture of success was too tempting to ignore and many were lured into the field. Among them were two renowned characters. They performed so well, and with such stylized effectiveness, Spanish shipping and coastal fortifications began to know that Hawkins and Drake were at work. Their annoyances to the King of Spain prompted Philip II to tell the Queen of England that her roaming "bad boys" in the "Spanish Main" had exceeded their welcome, and she had to do something about their unrestricted highjacking. Inasmuch as Hawkins and Drake were doing a man's job, with some obscure special favor in her behalf, the Queen quietly sustained their behavior and made no direct accusations, but openly for everyone to hear, she made loud and vitriolic condemnations against their contemptuous performances in the Caribbean. King Philip could hardly accept such a piece of obscure diplomacy and its feeble appeasement. However, it didn't matter so very much— Spain received a ghastly defeat with the destruction of the Spanish Armada, and brought to Spain's far-flung possessions in the Caribbean grievous tidings—her protection of them would henceforth be lessened. Jamaica was exposed to harassing raiders in helpless and precarious torment. Her security was challenged—it worried her!

The French and English ships roaming the Caribbean were there on special business, and further outcries for help from Spain by Jamaica were gagged, and the trade winds moaned the excru-

The retiring storm; woman collecting sea food on the beach at low tide.

ciating denials in the ears of brooding and helpless islanders. Jamaica couldn't starve, so she resorted to extreme pressure on her slaves to perform miracles in the fields. She became reliant upon slavery and herself became enslaved in the attempt to ward off starvation.

Sir Henry Morgan sensed the conditions in the West Indies and went out to give them a test. He apparently probed in the right places because his attacks won for him immediate fortunes wherever he struck—all in the name of patriotism for England. Rumors had it that his activities were slightly short of outright piracy.

In 1649 the head of Charles I became an anatomical specimen of detachment. Oliver Cromwell lost no time striking at his adversaries, in particular the Roman Catholic Church and anything Spanish. His ambitions made themselves felt with no penitent aversions to the pain his actions might cause. Swiftly he turned to Jamaica, where he tore the remnants of Spanish rule from its deteriorating anchorage and sent the Spaniards scurrying over the Diablo mountains, and down to defeat at Ocho Rios. At Runaway Bay the survivors managed to scramble into small boats, turned their noses towards Cuba and shoved off. Among the tattered and mildewed flags sat the dejected Don Arnaldo de Sasi, the last Spanish governor of Jamaica! That was the year 1660 and it also was the year of Jamaica's renascence.

Thirty-two years later, Port Royal, situated on the end of a long arm of land protecting Kingston harbor, had gained world renown by its aptitude for putting up with wickedness. It was the gathering place of rich planters, spendthrifts, waterlogged sailors, ad-

Market gossips at Brown's Town where every variety of produce indigenous to Jamaica is offered for sale.

venturers, and buccaneers. All of them sought the conviviality of social wrecks. The human dregs and the sots were received enthusiastically by the distaff members of the human race who joined in their trickeries, listened attentively to plots of murder and rich braggadocio. Since none suffered from impecuniosity, the dissipations must have been beyond anyone's conjecture.

On June 7, 1692, the raucous laughter and gabble of hundreds of people suddenly ended when a tremendous earthquake shook most of Port Royal off the tip of land upon which it stood, and slipped it into the churning Caribbean. The remnant of Port Royal, after reconstruction, was destroyed in 1703 by fire. Henceforth the city, the imbroglio of wickedness, was bereft of its unique reputation. Ships entering Kingston harbor today invariably sense a slight list to starboard—many crowd the rails hoping to see the graveyard of Port Royal.

Along the coast of Jamaica enormous estates appeared, for the most part under cultivation. They belonged to English emigrants holding lavish land grants. Europe wanted sugar, and Jamaica was the right place to grow cane. Every demand upon Jamaica's expediency to meet the needs abroad was honored, but this was effected through the use of black and white slaves. The latter were outcasts from the British Isles who had skirmishes with the law.

Thus another kind of gold manifested its importance with roots deep in the soil of Jamaica. The bones of Columbus, wherever they rested, relaxed and in permanent alignment, were unaware of the significance that Green bore to Gold—the Spaniards were painfully color-blind.

"Crabs to buy." Edible and delicious food for the epicurean and the hungry, sealed in "nature's tins."

PHILIP KAPPEL

The departure of the Spaniards from Jamaica gave their former slaves the golden opportunity to escape into the rough terrain and safely hide in the heart of a strange assemblage of steep conical mountains surrounded by sink holes that went deep into the heart of the island. A more formidable barrier against intruders or being discovered would be impossible to duplicate. This region on maps today is called the Cockpit Country in the Parish of Trelawny. Without roads, the penetration of the area by pursuers met with feeble success, and thus the Maroons, the former Spanish slaves, enlivened their well-being with a feeling of security and without bondage to anyone. To this very day the descendants of the Maroons enjoy self-rule and tax-free lands. Many bands of the Maroons fled to the northeastern part of the Blue Mountains and differed from the others by being incompatible with the rough conduct for which the Maroons in the Cockpit Country were notably disposed, making frequent sorties into the surrounding countryside to steal provisions by any method that would expedite their needs. The Blue Mountain groups lived in quiet domesticity and enjoyed the rewards of their industry in the fields that made them self-sufficient. In their region the planters found that coffee trees grew well. After the introduction of coffee on the slopes of the Blue Mountains in 1728, its fame as exceptional coffee spread around the world.

The Maroons in the Cockpit Country eventually exhausted the patience of the Jamaicans. Their contumelious performances were countermanded with strong-armed resistance by Edward Trelawny, who was Governor of Jamaica in 1738. He sent his troops

The man from Cayman Island describes the way an ornery sea-turtle is lured to a colorful decoy from which there is no happy ending.

into the tangle of jungle growth in pursuit of the culprits. Enough was enough and he wisely concluded the search with the offer of a treaty. The concessions pleased the Maroons and for a short time there was peace. But peace in the rest of the world became a very involved accumulation of general hates and strained relations. Spain and England had individual differences, and not to leave the French out of the picture it must be remembered that England was locked in war with that nation for seven years that began in 1756. It was not until Spain in 1762 threw her fighting equipment in with that of France that Jamaica had imposing problems again to worry her on a world-wide scale. Even in those days it became apparent that distances made small comfort when much-needed supplies from the mother country were intercepted.

Jamaica was south of Cuba, where the people were well fed and rich. Ninety miles of open sea, more or less, made all the difference between plenty and want, and it was not chance deliberation that brought to Cuba the sting of a hit and run invasion that netted Jamaica a treasure trove of gold from Havana and much-needed supplies for her people.

After the Peace of Paris, George III began to notice dissension in the American Colonies—something concerned with such poppy-cock as "taxation without representation" which was brushed aside and allowed to simmer. It was a shock to him when the "tea" was scuttled in Boston harbor and the kettle of discontentment blew up into a full-fledged revolution, sending Paul Revere out into the night armed with a prearranged signal "flash"—"one if by land and two if by sea"—and Paul Revere stabled a mighty tired horse after his ride.

Retarded prosperity—Harmony Vale, Edinburgh Castle, Pedro District, St. Ann.

PHILIP KAPPEL

The year 1775 gave George III some severe headaches. The caldron of discontentment began to take on fresh significance—France, Spain, and Holland rushed forward with their dippers to join the Americans who were already at the punch bowl of war. Fortified with their drink of distilled derisions and cachinnations against England, they retired to the chart rooms to plan the course of her destruction, but Englishmen had something to say about that and went into the fray outnumbered. Jamaica became a pawn again and bemoaned her poor luck. This time the war put tremendous trade losses squarely into her lap. Her customers in the American Colonies were among the best she had.

The French fleet in the West Indies made very certain that Jamaica's welfare was of paramount importance to her and proceeded to strangle the island's trade routes. Any attempt to break out ran up against a near perfect seal, for the time being: Nelson, with brilliant qualifications, was put in charge of Fort Charles at Port Royal. England also strengthened every notable fort on the island. The indomitable Admiral Rodney, in command of the British fleet in the West Indies, made a speedy attack on the Dutch Colonies and very soon bolstering supplies began to appear in Jamaica, where the dwindling reserves were dangerously low. Rodney then set sail in haste from his anchorage at St. Lucia, where news was received that the Spanish fleet was going to be joined by the French in order to subdue Jamaica. He intercepted the French fleet and inflicted a devastating blow—it was a complete victory south of Guadeloupe and broke up further destructionist threats, which gave Jamaica a breathing spell; the year 1782 had some bright moments of good fortune for the island.

Maroon girl of Comfort Castle, Moore Town, Portland. For two shillings the stem of bananas was ours; the smile sealed the bargain.

PHILIP KAPPEL

With the Peace of Versailles in 1783, hostilities ceased between England and her former American Colonies but another evil awoke and this time in nearby Haiti. Three words, Liberty, Equality, and Fraternity, carried on banners and in the hearts of Frenchmen during the French Revolution, began to sink into the consciousness of the Haitian slaves, who demanded immediate restitution to a world of freedoms. Because their request was too long in being granted they resolved to do something about it the hard way and promptly made mincemeat of their overlords, and then turned upon their plantations and destroyed them too. Fired with such zeal the slaves were ready to attack anyone who stood in their way and terror broke out among the white inhabitants of Haiti, who fled to the shores of Jamaica in large numbers. Such an exodus was bound to give the slaves in Jamaica something to think about and what they thought over was putting an end to their own enslavement. In the meanwhile the situation in Haiti was being watched with deep interest.

By a succession of eliminations, Christophe emerged as the undisputed leader of the slaves in Haiti. With sweeping boldness he challenged Napoleon to come over to Haiti and reverse the course the slaves embarked upon towards a new order for themselves and the island. He then retired to his fortifications at Cap-Haïtien to wait for the great man who destroyed whole armies across the face of Europe. When Napoleon never came it was interpreted as a sign of weakness; this also motivated the Maroons, in the Cockpit Country, to exercise their customary restlessness and insolence, which forced the authorities to grant them fresh concessions while

Cleaning ginger in the District Known by the Name of Look-Behind, edge of the Cockpit Country in south Trelawny.

PHILIP KAPPEL

the Jamaican slaves remained in tight custody of their overlords in sullen deportment.

In 1805, Napoleon, who bitterly resented the action of Christophe, decided to liquidate some special hates; since he had little love for Jamaica she was in line for a battering too. Thus, the parvenu and hero of Europe, let's say so far, executed his plans with cunning deployment, and suddenly his fleet appeared in the West Indies. British fighting ships on duty in the Caribbean now had the chance to prove to the Jamaicans that the expense of provisioning the ships with such hardship as they protested from time to time was going to pay off with liberal dividends. Jamaica, well aware of the threat to her fragile security, turned about face and vociferously gave the British fleet her blessings. Nelson, buoyant with confidence, raced towards the French fleet, to which he gave chase soon after the ravishing of Dominica, and caught up with the ships at Trafalgar, where he defeated the combined fleets of France and Spain, thus ending further worriment from them.

If improvement was noticed in Jamaica's status, many aspects of her well-being were still plagued by slavery, which became a topic of persistent interest to Englishmen at home. The miasma of slavery overwhelmed any sweetness left in its favor, and a law was enacted in England by 1807 that made it a felony to carry slaves in British ships or import them into British possessions.

Henceforth, thoughts turned ardently towards measures of restoration, especially towards trade. The magnetism of sugar enticed to Jamaica ships from everywhere and they returned to their respective home ports to release the news about the new order in

Wash day: a running stream, a quiet pool, and a place to bleach clothes in the sunshine.

PHILIP KAPPEL

Jamaica. It soon became common knowledge that the former slaves received absolute liberation in 1838.

It is in excess of a hundred years since the transition and change came to Jamaica. Providence has a kindly way of preparing people for great alterations and our modern era is not devoid of great changes in the process of formulation; we are beset by them in one way or another. If they are in evidence anywhere, they are bound to appear in Jamaica also. The *avant garde* of modern times are here, and couldn't be less conspicuous. If the glitter of our age is making a striking demonstration, the youth and the elder statesmen have the weapons today with which to fashion the respectability and the improvement of their people.

The globe has shrunk—contact with a world that is constantly sending to Jamaica cultural and commercial emissaries, by air and sea, makes available the "yardstick" with which to measure the size and the abilities of the garrulous and the worker. Their aptitudes will procreate the leadership of tomorrow; in a land blessed with so much of nature's generosity, any transgressions and abuse would be strictly man-made.

I should like to offer this book, and everything it represents, as the ensemble of the author's wanderings in the island of Jamaica; and whomsoever the charm of the island has also enjoined in fellowship, the chain of enduring fascination will forever be his enslavement.

These pictures represent the exposure of life as it appeared to the artist, without adulteration and departure from the tempo and stark fascination so worthy of documentation. In all consciousness,

Jamaica store at Alexandria. Patient donkeys await the unloading of their hampers filled with yams, yampees, and sweet potatoes.

PHILIP KAPPEL

it was the intention of the artist to race against time, to arrest the charm of Jamaica before further changes inflicted upon the quintessence of the island's simplicity, the modifications that they impose upon the character of the land. These pages also represent many personal experiences as observer and guest. Though many are omitted due to the limitations of publication, they are, nevertheless, recorded where recollections are permanently kept—where happy times and moments of abandonment are bound into the heart with the memories of gracious friends and friendly strangers.

PHILIP KAPPEL
New Milford, Connecticut

Indian steers drawing sugar cane wagon to the factory. Richmond-Llandovery, Laughlands.

PHILIP KAPPEL